NML/lt

KU-825-515

KID

Kid

SIMON ARMITAGE

ff

faber and faber

First published in 1992
by Faber and Faber Limited
Bloomsbury House
74-77 Great Russell Street
London WC1B 3DA
This special Poetry Firsts edition first published in 2010

Typeset by Wilmaset Limited, Wirral
Printed and bound in the UK by CPI Mackays, Chatham

A CIP record for this book
is available from the British Library

ISBN 978-0-571-25930-4

2 4 6 8 10 9 7 5 3 1

Contents

Acknowledgements

Acknowledgements and thanks are due to the editors of the following publications in which some of these poems first appeared: *Bête Noire, The Echo Room, Joe soap's canoe, Lampshade, London Magazine, The North, Other Poetry, Orbis, Poetry (Chicago), Poetry Book Society Anthology 1990/1, Poetry Review, Responses, Rialto, Slow Dancer, Scratch, Smoke, Spectator, Sunday Times, Swansea Review, Times Literary Supplement, Verse,* and *The Wide Skirt.*

Gooseberry Season

Which reminds me. He appeared
at noon, asking for water. He'd walked from town
after losing his job, leaving a note for his wife and his brother
and locking his dog in the coal bunker.
We made him a bed

and he slept till Monday.
A week went by and he hung up his coat.
Then a month, and not a stroke of work, a word of thanks,
a farthing of rent or a sign of him leaving.
One evening he mentioned a recipe

for smooth, seedless gooseberry sorbet
but by then I was tired of him: taking pocket money
from my boy at cards, sucking up to my wife and on his last night
sizing up my daughter. He was smoking my pipe
as we stirred his supper.

Where does the hand become the wrist?
Where does the neck become the shoulder? The watershed
and then the weight, whatever turns up and tips us over that
    razor's edge
between something and nothing, between
one and the other.

I could have told him this
but didn't bother. We ran him a bath
and held him under, dried him off and dressed him
and loaded him into the back of the pick-up.
Then we drove without headlights

to the county boundary,
dropped the tailgate, and after my boy
had been through his pockets we dragged him like a mattress
across the meadow and on the count of four
threw him over the border.

This is not general knowledge, except
in gooseberry season, which reminds me, and at the table
I have been known to raise an eyebrow, or scoop the sorbet
into five equal portions, for the hell of it.
I mention this for a good reason.

True North

Hitching home for the first time, the last leg
being a bummed ride in a cold guard's van
through the unmanned stations to a platform
iced with snow. It's not much to crow about,

the trip from one term at Portsmouth Poly,
all that Falklands business still to come. From there
the village looked stopped; a clutch of houses
in a toy snow-storm with the dust settled

and me ready to stir it, loaded up
with a haul of new facts, half expecting
flags or bunting, a ticker-tape welcome,
a fanfare or a civic reception.

In the Old New Inn two men sat locked
in an arm-wrestle – their one combined fist
dithered like a compass needle. Later,
after Easter, they would ask me outside

for saying Malvinas in the wrong place
at the wrong time, but that night was Christmas
and the drinks were on them. Christmas! At home
I hosted a new game: stretch a tissue

like a snare drum over a brandy glass,
put a penny on, spark up, then take turns
to dimp burning cigs through the diaphragm
before the tissue gives, the penny drops.

As the guests yawned their heads off I lectured
about wolves: how they mass on the shoreline
of Bothnia, wait for the weather, then
make the crossing when the Gulf heals over.

Brassneck

United, mainly,
every odd Saturday,
or White Hart Lane for a worthwhile away game.
Down in the crowds at the grounds where the bread is:
the gold, the plastic,
the cheque-books, the readies,

the biggest fish
or the easiest meat,
or both. Consider that chap we took last week:
we turned him over and walked off the terrace
with a grand exactly
in dog-eared tenners;

takings like that
don't get reported.
Carter, he's a sort of junior partner;
it's two seasons now since we first teamed up
in the Stretford End
in the FA Cup;

it was all United
when I caught him filching
my cigarette case, and he felt me fishing
a prial of credit cards out of his britches.
Since that day
we've worked these pitches.

We tend to kick off
by the hot dog vans
and we've lightened a good many fair-weather fans
who haven't a clue where to queue for tickets.
Anything goes, if it's
loose we lift it.

At City last year
in the derby match
we did the right thing with a smart-looking lass
who'd come unhitched in the crush from her friend.
We escorted her out
of the Platt Lane End,

arm in arm
along the touchline,
past the tunnel and out through the turnstile
and directed her on to a distant police car.
I did the talking
and Carter fleeced her.

As Carter once put it:
when we're on the ball
we can clean someone out, from a comb to a coil,
and we need nine eyes to watch for the coppers
though at Goodison Park
when I got collared

two bright young bobbies
took me into the toilets
and we split the difference. Bent policemen;
there's always a couple around when you need them.
It's usually Autumn
when we loosen our fingers

at the Charity Shield
which is pretty big business
though semis and finals are birthdays and Christmas.
Hillsborough was a different ball game of course;
we'd started early,
then saw what the score was,

so we turned things in
as a mark of respect,
just kept enough back to meet certain expenses
(I'm referring here to a red and blue wreath;
there are trading standards,
even among thieves).

Carter keeps saying
he'd be quick to wager
that worse things go on in the name of wages,
but I've let Carter know there's a place and a time
to say as we speak,
speak as we find.

Speaking of Carter,
and not that I mind,
he thinks I'm a touch on the gingery side:
my voice a little too tongued and grooved,
my locks a little
too washed and groomed,

my cuticles tenderly
pushed back and pruned,
both thumbnails capped with a full half-moon,
each fingernail manicured, pared and polished ...
We can work hand in hand if we stick to the rules:
he keeps his cunt-hooks out of my wallet,
I keep my tentacles
out of his pocket.

Shrove Tuesday

That evening, over pancakes, when you told me
it was not for love, not even for money

but just for the children,
then ran through those several other women,

I must have looked for all the world
like that lost, knocked-sideways, bowled-over girl

who, at odds of more than
a hundred-thousand-million

to one,
had come

so far but never dropped across
the word or the idea of snow. Then there it was

one morning, acid-white and waiting
as she reeled back the bedroom curtain,

the lawn and the street,
the whole picture ankle-deep

and crisp and even and still snowing.
Incredibly, she was twenty-something.

Wintering Out

To board six months
at your mother's place, pay
precious little rent
and not lift a finger, don't think
for a minute I'm moaning.

It's a doll's house end-terrace
with all the trimmings: hanging baskets,
a double garage,
a rambling garden with
a fairy-tale ending and geese

on the river. Inside
it's odd, dovetailed into next door
with the bedrooms
back-to-back, wallpaper walls
so their phone calls ring out

loud and clear
and their footsteps on the stairs
run up and down like the practice scales
of a Grade 1 cornet lesson:
their daughter's. From day one

I've been wondering, from the morning
I hoisted the blind
and found
your mother on the lawn
in a housecoat and leggings

expertly skewering fallen fruit
with the outside tine
of the garden fork,
then casting it off, overboard
into the river. I've said

nothing, held my breath
for a whole season, waited
like Johnny Weismuller
under the ice, held on
to surface in a new house, our own

where the wood
will be treated and buffed and the grain
will circle like weather
round the knots
of high pressure. Here

we've had to button it: not fly
off the handle or stomp upstairs
yelling *That's it you bastard*
and sulk for a week
over nothing. Here

the signs are against us:
some fluke
in the spring water
turning your golden hair lime-green, honey.
Even the expert

from Yorkshire Water
taking pH tests
and fur from the kettle
can't put his finger on it.
We'll have to go; leave

the bathroom with
no lock, the door that opens
of its own accord, the frostless glass
and pretty curtains
that will not meet.

It only takes one night,
your mother
having one of her moments, out
at midnight
undercoating the gutter to catch us

in the bath, fooling around
in Cinemascope. Nothing for it but to dip
beneath the bubbles,
take turns to breathe through the tube
of the loofah, sit tight

and wait for summer.

Looking for Weldon Kees

I'd heard it said by Michael Hofmann
that *Collected Poems* would blow my head off,
but,
    being out of print
    and a hot potato,
    it might be a hard one
    to get hold of;
more than a case of shopping and finding
nothing on the shelves between Keats and Kipling.

There was too much water under the Golden Gate
since the day that dude became overrated,
the dawn
    he locked both doors
    of his Tudor Ford
    and took one small step
    off the face of the planet.
No will, no note, no outline of police chalk
on the deck around his drainpipes and overcoat,

not even a whiff of spontaneous combustion
to hang his vaporizing act on. Simultaneously, Robinson,
who
    had been through the hostel
    with a host of problems,
    was back in town
    and giving me the runaround.
We went back years, me and that man Robinson,
the illiterate son of a Maltese policeman

who'd arrived by boat in 'sixty-three, broke,
and made a name for himself by deed poll
which
     he wrote as Mr X
     when he signed in –
     or the Maltese cross
     as we christened him.
Since we first shook hands we'd had more ups and downs
than San Francisco, and I'd heard he'd gone south;

but his monogram daubed on my car windscreen,
his pidgin English on my answering machine,
that
     Malteser propped
     in my letter box,
     it all made sense:
     it was Mr X
a.k.a. Robinson, his cryptic APB turning up
like confetti long after the cake had been cut.

So what? Well, a long running ad in the TLS
starred the Book Finding Service's finest points,
including:
       • No task too great
       • Free O/P search
       • Personal attention
       and their number in Brighton.
After 1 p.m. I made the connection, and dialled,
and their rarities section asked me to wait, so I held,

and I heard the tip of an index finger
running down and along a ready reckoner,
then
     a different noise
     as I gave my order
     and an obovoid
     of screwed-up paper
got lobbed into a litter basket. Evidently
American books were of a different kidney.

On the same split second I replaced the receiver
the telephonist buzzed and I couldn't believe her:
it was
     Robinson,
     in reception.
     I burst through
     to a waiting room
devoid of everything but his body odour
and also, as bold as the mark of Zorro,

X marked the spot where he'd taken the trouble
to felt-tip his name in the circular table.
I studied
     the blasé slash
     of his autograph,
     the pair of obliques
     joined up at the feet,
the two loose ends like the lace of a shoe
from which a full name might step out or undo.

Underneath, a parcel, wrapped in a bin-bag,
about the size and weight of a book, a hardback.
No point
       unrolling it,
       disclosing it,
       making a fuss
       or blowing things up,
and that night as I chanced it through the subway
I thought I made out Robinson ahead of me.

The Catch

Forget
the long, smouldering
afternoon. It is

this moment
when the ball scoots
off the edge

of the bat; upwards,
backwards, falling
seemingly

beyond him
yet he reaches
and picks it

out
of its loop
like

an apple
from a branch,
the first of the season.

Robinson in Two Cities

Cities of architecture and scaffolding, tower blocks
taking the temperature, external elevator-cars outpacing
window-cleaning cages, projects and broken deadlines, Robinson

near the station. All routes end here. Cities of junctions
and ring roads, inside lanes peeling off to the left
shunting traffic into neighbourhoods, districts, Robinson

on the loop bus, his third lap. Cranes making the skyline.
Cities of offences against the person, taxis and sirens
and crossing the street from nowhere to nowhere, Robinson

on foot. Cities at dusk, each outpointing the other
with starlings. A choice of evening papers, the bridge,
and later with his tightrope act along the ledge, Robinson

in two minds.

You May Turn Over and Begin ...

'Which of these films was Dirk Bogarde
not in? One hundredweight of bauxite

makes how much aluminium?
How many tales in *The Decameron*?'

General Studies, the upper sixth, a doddle, a cinch
for anyone with an ounce of common sense

or a calculator
with a memory feature.

Having galloped through but not caring enough
to check or double-check, I was dreaming of

milk-white breasts and nakedness, or more specifically
virginity.

That term – everybody felt the heat
but the girls were having none of it:

long and cool like cocktails,
out of reach, their buns and pigtails

only let out for older guys with studded jackets
and motor-bikes and spare helmets.

One jot of consolation
was the tall spindly girl riding pillion

on her man's new Honda
who, with the lights at amber,

put down both feet and stood to stretch her limbs,
to lift the visor and push back her fringe

and to smooth her tight jeans.
As he pulled off down the street

she stood there like a wishbone,
high and dry, her legs wide open,

and rumour has it he didn't notice
till he came round in the ambulance

having underbalanced on a tight left-hander.
A Taste of Honey. Now I remember.

At Sea

It is not through weeping,
but all evening the pale blue eye
on your most photogenic side has kept
its own unfathomable tide. Like the boy
at the dyke I have been there:

held out a huge finger,
lifted atoms of dust with the point
of a tissue and imagined slivers of hair
in the oil on the cornea. We are both
in the dark, but I go on

drawing the eyelid up by its lashes,
folding it almost inside-out, then finding
and hiding every mirror in the house
as the iris, besieged with the ink
of blood rolls back

into its own orbit. Nothing
will help it. Through until dawn
you dream the true story of the boy
who hooked out his eye and ate it,
so by six in the morning

I am steadying the ointment
that will bite like an onion, piping
a line of cream while avoiding the pupil
and in no time it is glued shut
like a bad mussel.

Friends call round
and mean well. They wait
and whisper in the air-lock of the lobby
with patches, eyewash, the truth
about mascara.

Even the cats are on to it;
they bring in starlings, and because their feathers
are the colours of oil on water in sunlight
they are a sign of something.
In the long hours

beyond us, irritations heal
into arguments. For the eighteenth time
it comes to this: the length of your leg sliding out
from the covers, the ball of your foot
like a fist on the carpet

while downstairs
I cannot bring myself to hear it.
Words have been spoken; things that were bottled
have burst open and to walk in now
would be to walk in

on the ocean.

Fire

We could not see it from the cemetery
but now, on the bottom road, there is smoke.
Pull up; let's stumble over this rough ground
and look on it: the extent, the damage.

Women: this evening they are in our hair.
We rub our eyes and see them. Friend, I heard
you stood two ironing boards top to toe
so it wouldn't get boring. What went wrong?
Betty lost her baby so she dug out

her eye. The blood. Let's back off. Like bluebells
let's nod or shake just as the breeze blows: yes,
they seem to have it under control; no,
from the cemetery we could not see it.

Mr Robinson's Holiday

As if gravity had brought him here, down
through the matrix of the minor counties
to the South West where the mainland dips its toe
in the ocean. From the cliff, with the viewfinder,

Robinson trained on a seal in the bay coming up
like a spaceman. And in the guesthouse,
Robinson giving a bogus address, not wanting
the landlord's friends to visit his place, force

the window casements, try on his wardrobe
in the full-length mirror, load up with photographs
and tapes or help themselves to a cooked breakfast.
Robinson thinking this is ridiculous, Robinson.

One word about the weather: uncertain. One sock
in his coat pocket, that's odd, and for the upkeep
of this private shore, Robinson slotting a hermit crab
in the honesty-box. Time on his hands:

Robinson at the beach, baking slowly like a loaf
for hours, shaking down behind the windbreak,
then all evening finding sand running out
from unlikely places. The mark where his watch was –

a good day's work, Robinson. As for St Michael's Mount
he would rather die than pay the ferryman, and
in the hour before high tide on the flooded causeway –
Robinson ghost-like and up to his neck in it.

Look, it is overwhelming; the air at St Ives
so good he could take a slice and frame it,
and this the town where the smell of fish
once stopped a clock. Robinson not one

for taking things lightly, not one for caution
on those roller-coasting lanes over the coves and inlets.
Robinson's radio – good news on the weather front:
sunshine mainly with bulletins of rain.

At the stately home, his boots impounded for a pair
of plastic overshoes, then warned for touching this
and brushing that and nudging the other. Robinson
to himself: unclean, unclean. Back at the room,

Robinson damned if he'll pay an extra pound
for a plug for the bath, soaking for an hour at least
with his heel in the hole. Then without a towel
drying off on the curtain. Typical, Robinson. Typical.

Awake all night, a man in the next room coughing
like a seal. Down on the shore the moon like a torch;
whichever way he walks it finds him, follows him,
will not flinch when he spins round to surprise it,

and in that way reminds him.

Alaska

So you upped
and went. Big deal!
Now you must be sitting pretty.
Now you must see me
like a big kodiak bear,

safe and holed up
for the close season, then rumbled.
Girl, you must see me
like the crown prince
rattling

round his icy palace,
the cook and bottle-washer gone,
snuck off, a moonlight flit
to the next estate
for sick pay, wages, running water

in their own chambers, that type
of concession. Girl,
you must picture me: clueless,
the brand of a steam iron
on my dress shirt,

the fire left on all night,
the kitchen a scrap heap
of ring-pulls and beer cans
but let me say, girl,
the only time I came within a mile

of missing you
was a rainy Wednesday, April,
hauling in the sheets,
trying to handle
that big king-sizer. Girl,

you should see yourself with him,
out in the snowfield
like nodding donkeys
or further west, you and him,
hand in hand,

his and hers,
and all this
under my nose,
like the Bering Strait,
just a stone's throw away.

Untitled, with Flowers

At the Working Men's Home Produce Auction
we pick up six prize cactus dahlias
for a song. These are our first real flowers
and like new parents we nurse them back home
to a warm house without a single vase.

Idiots! Four will stand in a bottle,
its neck pinching the stalks, those stilts which launch
the blooms – pink pom-pom sea anemones.
The other two? A brain wave! We stand them
in the loo. Like kids in a balloon trip
they lean out over the seat, wanting to see
and be seen, waiting to be pointed out.

At 6 a.m., full of booze, I lumber
into the bathroom. Declined, top heavy,
they have lost height, jettisoned their petals,
the tight-incurved cusps – lifeboats below them –
evidence of weeping. They surprise me.

Poem

And if it snowed and snow covered the drive
he took a spade and tossed it to one side.
And always tucked his daughter up at night.
And slippered her the one time that she lied.

And every week he tipped up half his wage.
And what he didn't spend each week he saved.
And praised his wife for every meal she made.
And once, for laughing, punched her in the face.

And for his mum he hired a private nurse.
And every Sunday taxied her to church.
And he blubbed when she went from bad to worse.
And twice he lifted ten quid from her purse.

Here's how they rated him when they looked back:
sometimes he did this, sometimes he did that.

The Guilty

They look us dead in the eye
and deny it. They turn out their pockets –
nothing but biscuits and the shreds of a tissue.
They will undress their children this very minute.

Suggest their names, they are astonished.
Push them, they remember dates and places. Push them
further, they come up with blood groups, postcodes,
distinguishing features. Their curtains twitch

when we call round in the car, or we hear them
leaving like rabbits through the back door.

They take on habits, the guilty; throw us
from the scent. Analogue watches worn to the inside,
the buttering of bread before the slicing.
They let out their belts, one notch,

before eating; salt their supper before they taste it
and flush it twice if they flush the toilet.
Shake their hands, their hands are like putty.
Their children agree with them, absolutely.

So when shall we birch these people?
And how do we know these things?

Judge Chutney's Final Summary

Members
of the jury,
you have surfed

the tidal wave,
listened
with patience,

held out
against the avalanche
of evidence

and now
I admit it.
I am guilty.

Accept it,
it is overwhelming.
Acts of Parliament

move in on me
like glaciers,
I have taken guidelines

for tramlines
and have followed
trains of thought

into overgrown sidings
or coasted, out of steam,
to a halt

against the incline.
I have rambled
through scrub

telling the trees
from the wood, eaten
alibis for breakfast,

spotted lies
like breadcrumbs
but arrived

in a ghost town
where one fat magpie
looks up

and goes on feeding.
Vapour trails
dissolve like rainbows.

I have picked up
and hauled in
a line of inquiry,

the thread
of a story
which ends in my hands

with the head
of a viper;
or I have swallowed it –

thought of a number
and doubled it.
Letting the tail

fit the punishment
has been a case
of pinning the crime

on the biggest donkey.
To retract,
to take it

all back
would mean unpicking
every stitch

in every sentence.
God help me.
I have looked

long and hard,
lost the ball
in the sun,

thrown the wheat out
with the chaff
and once,

in a strong wind,
winnowed a baby
from its bath.

Remember that?
Members
of the jury,

I have reached
a verdict
on which

you are all concurring:
life
to mean life, life

to mean living.
Finally then,
I, Chutney,

being tired of mind
and tired of body
leave you this:

the truth
and nothing but the truth, plus
all my worldly goods.

What do I hear
for this first exhibit:
the moon

from the millpond
which I lifted this evening
like a wheel of cheese?

Or a tablecloth
out from under a banquet.
Or a saucer of cream.

Or the skin
from a pudding.
I have packed a suitcase,

let me open the bidding.
What do I hear?
What will you give me?

Look, Stranger

Skimmed into the sea of the century
you went well but fell short of the far shore.
Now we see it in terms of that journey,
the stone skipping over the waves of war.

Where it sank it bedded down and formed:
sandbar, reef, atoll. Now it's an island;
boats set out from it in treacherous storms,
telescopes strain to pick out the mainland.

The first to cross find a coast of sharp rocks,
sheer cliffs, high tides and a dangerous swell.
A branch, like a vine, trails down from the top –
they start to climb, then stop; they know that smell:

Audacious audacious could be the root,
but commonly this tree's known by its fruit.

Kid

Batman, big shot, when you gave the order
to grow up, then let me loose to wander
leeward, freely through the wild blue yonder
as you liked to say, or ditched me, rather,
in the gutter ... well, I turned the corner.
Now I've scotched that 'he was like a father
to me' rumour, sacked it, blown the cover
on that 'he was like an elder brother'
story, let the cat out on that caper
with the married woman, how you took her
downtown on expenses in the motor.
Holy robin-redbreast-nest-egg-shocker!
Holy roll-me-over-in-the-clover,
I'm not playing ball boy any longer
Batman, now I've doffed that off-the-shoulder
Sherwood-Forest-green and scarlet number
for a pair of jeans and crew-neck jumper;
now I'm taller, harder, stronger, older.
Batman, it makes a marvellous picture:
you without a shadow, stewing over
chicken giblets in the pressure cooker,
next to nothing in the walk-in larder,
punching the palm of your hand all winter,
you baby, now I'm the real boy wonder.

Never Mind the Quality:

feel the width.
But how many times
had she worked the blade
of a paper-scraper
under a loose length
of faded paper and pulled,
only to see it shear,
or tear, or taper out

like the roots of a tree
or the source of a river?
More times than she cared
to remember. Of all days
it was Sunday.
One small corner
of the parlour wall
had peeled away

and she folded it back
like the finishing touch
to a well-made bed,
then took it in hand
and simply she used
her own weight, leant right out
like a wind-surfer rounding
the tip of Cape Horn

and it came
and kept coming, breathtaking,
like a seam of ore
through an unclaimed mountain –
from the skirting board
to the picture rail,
from the door frame
to the bay window.

Her man was adamant;
he would not have it
in the house,
would not dream of it.
Not on the creel
with his damp linen, no way.
Not near the hob
where his bread was rising,

not in the porch
where the grouse were hanging,
not on the couch, spread
like an antimacassar
of some measure.
In short, not nowhere.
Out it went, over the line
like a starched sheet

or an old tent
strung out for airing.
The word went round.
She of all people
had stripped a piece
the size of a bedspread.
A double bed
someone enlarged; a gable end

added another.
They gathered in the market
to trade stories,
held out their arms
as if it were
a fish, a pike, the one
that got away,
or so much cloth,

or a monster putt
from off the green – the ball
that teased the rim
of the cup then stopped
and dropped, sweet
as a nut, sunk.
The men could lip-read.
From their sinks and stoves

they looked up, undid
their aprons, kicked off
their slippers
and jumped in their brogues,
then slopped outside
with a bucket and brush
to swill down their flags
and watch their women.

It was dropping dark
and words were difficult
to see. 'This big, sisters,'
said one girl, her arms
and fingers spread, as if
relieved of a great cat's cradle
or ready for several feet
of fine imaginary yarn.

Abstracting Electricity

So that's that, global warming and the ozone hole
and how the season scorched the town's main reservoir
slowly down its backbone of benchmarks. Atlantis, we reckon,
as we wander through the crater and scratch around
half-heartedly for keepsakes, or hopscotch over the topsoil

which is broken and baked into perfect octagonal cakes.
There's an echo; let's talk for the sake of it. Language,
we know, is less use than half a scissor, so ramble on
past the bridge and the pumping-station where that life-buoy
hoopla-ed over the rain-gauge is a statement, and the shadows

of hang-gliders down in the valley are pterodactyls.
Or impress me with your first date, how he took you
to the rink but couldn't skate so you linked him
clockwise at a gentle pace. Later, unravelling
that sacred fiver from your grandmother's locket,

you stood the price of a pineapple sundae, two spoons,
and thawed out in the photo booth and split the prints –
your eyes gone red in the flash like the devil's.
Or blame it on a blip in your biorhythms:
how you're dead on your feet all day but at night

you can't unplug. A course of tablets does the trick
but your hair falls out in lumps so you dump it.
You take a job but it doesn't suit so you sack it.
You buy that car, a wreck with three months' tax and test
and tyres so bald that you drive on a penny and know

if it's heads or tails, the bonnet maloccluded from that brush
with the business end of a JCB, we lift both feet
when you run through a puddle; that bad. And the house:
remind me how you lapped copper wire round the meter, halved
the bills, hung shirts in the fridge from May to September.

And the platitudes: one standpipe doesn't make a summer,
the lead in a gallon of petrol wouldn't fill the teat
of a baby's bottle, which is small, though you wouldn't want it
as a wart at the end of your nose, sprung up overnight,
unsightly whichever side you see it from, unspeakable

but there on the tip of your tongue.

The Ornithologists

Keen spotters but wise about their habits
we watch closely for the season starting,
then trim the drainpipe with strips of plastic;
they catch the wind and scare off house martins.

The charm they bring to the eaves they nest in
doesn't change the price of disinfectant,
caustic soda or even sandblasting,
and the pile of money we might have spent

is safely tucked away or has been put
to better, brighter things. Tits and finches
are different, easier; we feed them nuts
and break the ice when the birdbath freezes.

It's how to live. Minds should be like houses:
clean, open, and in order like ours is.

Dear Robinson

You'd wake to the simple sounds of housework.
How I rose from that makeshift double-bed,
dressed in silence, then stacked the fire
without so much as stirring you, was beyond you.

From the far corner, twisting a duster
through the silverware, I'd watch as your eyes
became accustomed to the light. You'd smile;
I'd move on to the next precious object.

Robinson, a friend of a friend of mine
tells me you've been talking in a tone of voice
I don't much care for. A word of warning:
that morning when I sharpened a pencil

and spelt it out in capital letters, I meant it.
And another thing, darling: as I ran
my gently trembling tongue along the gummed edge
of the envelope, I was smiling.

East Riding

Seen by the lych-gate
pushing his bike,
then down near the goods yard
later that night.

Blond, freckled,
slightly asthmatic,
thought to be wearing
a corduroy jacket.

Friends and neighbours
are combing the sidings,
frogmen and dogs
will arrive in the morning.

A particular man
from Burton Agnes
is helping police
with their enquiries.

In Our Tenth Year

This book, this page, this harebell laid to rest
between these sheets, these leaves, if pressed still bleeds
a watercolour of the way we were.

Those years: the fuss of such and such a day,
that disagreement and its final word,
your inventory of names and dates and times,
my infantries of tall, dark, handsome lies.

A decade on, now we astound ourselves;
still two, still twinned but doubled now with love
and for a single night apart, alone,
how sure we are, each of the other half.

This harebell holds its own. Let's give it now
in air, with light, the chance to fade, to fold.
Here, take it from my hand. Now, let it go.

Ice

As if the window that will not close
and the bath water being barely hot enough
and the wet towels
were not enough to worry over.

But your favourite dress
is damp and unironed;
you haven't a stitch to wear
and I am to blame.

Now you will turn the house inside out.
Now you will tear through the wardrobe –
more shoes than Mrs Marcos, hangers
relieved of their shirts and blouses

till the armchair is constricted
with fabrics and colours
and the carpet alive
with cuffs, sleeves and collars.

I wait outside
by the fractured pipe
on the gable end
as the cream of your bath water

finds its way along the street
and turns the corner.
Already its edges
are beginning to harden.

About Ladybower

No cinefilm or snapshot could be trusted with this:
   the hatchback is a backyard
of severable parts, a curiosity shop of brackets, cogs,
   jockey wheels
and sprockets, the at ease components which fall in
   under monkey wrench
and allen key. Apparel is everything and today
   is no exception:
skintight lycra knickerbockers, trade vests, helmets,
   fingerless mittens
plus every optional appendage, every affordable et cetera
   that will button on
or batten down about our person as we catwalk
   the twenty-odd yards
from the portaloo back to the aforesaid Citroën
   to wheel out, and step up,
and push off around the gaggle of dumbstruck hikers.

Mountain bikes! Great horse bikes! Great chargers,
   unknackerable,
unstoppable, damn near unbuyable push-irons with a gear
   for every occasion.
After the preamble of tarmac, the small talking avenues
   we sidetrack a footpath
and are keen this time for the rolled-out chestnut paling
   of yesterday's ride,
the cleated bone-shaking walkway which end-stopped
   after a furlong

pitching us headlong, leaving us axle-high
    in a black peat soup
from which we hauled out, slogged back and sprang
    like blesboks
into the startled car park. But here the going is firm
    with traction to spare,
here bridleways are the watchwords and we talk
    as if they were elk trails
or ley lines or were underwritten by a network
    of waterways
which our handlebars might instinctively divine.

On the downslopes we sit tight, drop the seats,
    descend
at full tilt knowing full well the bikers' adage
    of 'what goes down
must lift again' – the zero average, the exact cancellation
    of climbing versus falling,
the upshot of which is to rise from the saddle
    and graft, to peruse
into gardens like cows over cattle truck tailgates
    or, in this garb,
basketballers: six-, seven-footers lolloping against the incline.
    Where you carve
through bog water two water wings rise up either side
    of the rear wheel,
carry you safe to the other side and in mulch or clay
    those toppings
bear out your competent tracks, mark your direction verbatim.
    In tow I wobble,
the apprentice funambulist trick-cycling that high wire,
    a relative dyslexic
where tracking, and pursuit, and tread-reading are concerned.

Undergrowth nods forward, chimes for a moment
in the spokes,
sticks its neck out and gets strimmed. Bent sticks
rear up like snakes
and are broken. One pot-hole cups the wheel and upends me.
Quickly the home straight,
the landing lights of cat's-eyes and too soon it is over,
one last long
kinematic free-wheel into the road's elbow, the whiplash
up and out
along the apron of the lake and a copybook quietness
to glide into.
In the Citroën we are overtaken: that numbness of skin,
limbs unreliable
like funny bones and the journey goes without saying.
It's clear now, the excess
worked up and ridden out. The animal in us exercised.

The Metaphor Now Standing at Platform 8

will separate at Birmingham New Street, and passengers
for the South West who sit for safety reasons in the rear carriages
will find themselves at Shit Creek Central without a paddle
or a valid ticket. No end of fancy talking will save them.

Parents and their children are today invited
to the engine of the metaphor, and may touch the dead man's
    handle.
Cow-catchers? Fried bacon on the footplateman's shovel?
    People,
please, this is 1990 not the Wild West.

You kids licking the tips of your pencils, I could talk
of the age of steam, riding the great Similitudes
into the record books. Take heart, a boy
could do worse than be a spotter of metaphors.

Here is the buffet car at the centre
of the metaphor, where hot buttered toast
and alcoholic beverages will certainly be mentioned.
In the next breath, lunch will be served.

This is not the allegorical boat train.
This is not the symbolic seaplane.
Madam, life is not a destination but a journey; sweet
that your friends should want to meet you there, but stupid.

Passengers, as part of our Transports of Delight programme
let me welcome this morning's poets. Beginning at the guard's van
they will troubadour the aisle reciting their short but engaging
   pieces.
Sir, I understand you have a reservation?

Feet off the seats, please. Lady, for the last time,
extinguish that cigarillo. This is a metaphor I'm running here
not a jamboree, and as soon as we get that straight
we're rolling. Till then, no one goes nowhere.

Song

The bridle-path, the river bank,
and where they crossed I took a length
of hazel bark, and carved a boat
no bigger than a fish, a trout,
and set it down and saw it float,
then sink. And where it sank
an inch of silver flesh declared itself
against the sun. Then it was gone.

And further south, beyond the bridge,
I took a nest of cotton grass
and flint to make a fire. Then watched
a thread of smoke unhook a pair
of seed propellers from a sycamore
which turned together and became
a dragonfly that drew the smoke
downstream. But the fire would not light.

Then at night, the house at the mouth
of the river. Inside, a fish,
a trout, the ounces of its soft
smoked meat prepared and on a plate.
I sat down there and ate. It is
the way of things, the taking shape
of things, beginning with their names;
secrets told in acts of sunlight,
promises kept by gifts of rain.

With the Tennessee Walking Horses

Nothing matters now;
not the pleats of my frock,
not the line or length

of my eyebrows
or whether I let my hair
fall this particular way

or that.
Not the letters from my mother.
Not the colour of the curtains.

If I listen – just the rattle
of cavessons somewhere outside
and the waterwheel, turning.

Then in the breaking-circle, him
with the Walking Horses.
I glare from the window

as he pivots, one hand checking
the tension of the lunge-rein,
the other collecting the slack

of his whip.
In the dry sand, each flick
of their hooves – a tight

controlled explosion.
I bite back each feeling
as it swells in my stomach.

Great Sporting Moments: The Treble

The rich! I love them. Trust them to suppose
the gift of tennis is deep in their bones.

Those chaps from the coast with all their own gear
from electric eyes to the umpire's chair,

like him whose arse I whipped with five choice strokes
perfected on West Yorkshire's threadbare courts:

a big first serve that strained his alloy frame,
a straight return that went back like a train,

a lob that left him gawping like a fish,
a backhand pass that kicked and drew a wisp

of chalk, a smash like a rubber bullet
and a bruise to go with it. Three straight sets.

Smarting in the locker rooms he offered
double or quits; he was a born golfer

and round the links he'd wipe the floor with me.
I played the ignoramus to a tee:

the pleb in the gag who asked the viscount
what those eggcup-like things were all about –

'They're to rest my balls on when I'm driving.'
'Blimey, guv, Rolls-Royce think of everything' –

but at the fifth when I hadn't faltered
he lost his rag and threw down the gauntlet;

we'd settle this like men: with the gloves on.
I said no, no, no, no, no, no, no. OK, come on then.

Robinson's Life Sentence

Rise early from a double bed,
take a shower, tie off the blind,
another dawn like open-heart surgery,
mosey downstairs, brew up, take time
over the papers, the results,
the notices, zip up, step out, bookworm
and browse down the high street,
pay for something by cheque or plastic,
see a man unhitch a sidecar
from his silver motorcycle, then
leave it there like a baby's shoe,
meet a friend, make a new friend,
take a drink, eat, talk shop,
re-string the steel guitar, scratch out
a new tune, try out someone's car for size,
buy oil or petrol by cheque or plastic,
make that call, write that card,
send out for supper, get stewed
on straight gin, turn in,
read a little, backpedal
through some old editions, crash out
and sleep like a bear, washed by wave
after wave of gentle dreams, but
wake again, and rise early.

Lines Thought to Have Been Written on the Eve of the Execution of a Warrant for His Arrest

Boys, I have a feeling in my water,
in my bones, that should we lose our houses
and our homes, our jobs, or just in general
come unstuck, she will not lend one button
from her blouse, and from her kitchen garden
not one bean. But through farmyards and dust bowls
we will lay down our topcoats, or steel ourselves
and bare our backs over streams and manholes.

Down Birdcage Walk in riots or wartime
we will not hear of her hitching her skirt
or see for ourselves that frantic footwork,
busy like a swan's beneath the surface.
But quickly our tank will stop in its tracks;
they'll turn the turret lid back like a stone;
inside, our faces set like flint, her name
cross-threaded in the barrels of our throats.

I have this from reliable sources:
boys, with our letters, our first class honours
and diplomas we are tenfold brighter
than her sons and daughters put together.
But someone hangs on every word they speak,
and let me mention here the hummingbird
that seems suspended at the orchid's lips,
or else the bird that picks the hippo's teeth.

Boys, if we burn, she will not pass one drop
of water over us, and if we drown
she will not let a belt or bootlace down,
or lend a hand. She'll turn instead and show
a leg, a stocking, sheer and ladderless.
And even then we will not lose our heads
by mouthing an air bubble out of turn
or spouting a smoke ring against her name.

But worse than this, in handouts and speeches
she will care for us, and cannot mean it.
Picture the stroke of the hour that takes her:
our faces will freeze as if the wind had changed,
we shall hear in our hearts a note, a murmur,
and talk in terms of where we stood, how struck,
how still we were the moment this happened,
in good faith, as if it really mattered.

8 p.m. and Raining When Robinson

arrives by bus in a town whose name
he would not care to mention,
sets his baggage down,
hails a taxi and pays a fiver, his heart
in his mouth, Robinson
saying, 'There's a road goes east, take it

for one mile then drop me. If there's change, you keep it.'
No names,
then, 'Hey, you're Robinson,
I saw that piece in the *Racing Post* ...' One mention
of himself and Robinson's heart
takes off with itself like a horse in a hailstorm, down

to the car park under the covered market, down
to that glove compartment where he left it ...
empty! Robinson's heart
goes down like an anchor. Mud now, his name,
and only minutes till they find him and mention
the million dollar question. 'Robinson,'

his doctor once told him, 'Robinson,
you should take things steady, son. Calm down.'
But his nerves, his hair, not to mention
his face looking more each day like a Photofit.
In heaven's name
they should finish him off but they haven't a heart

between them. Sprinting now, each beat of his heart
gazumping the next – take that, Robinson.
Someone drops his name
in a doorway, a body check brings him down,
they hold out his tongue and lean a blade against it:
'Next time you squeak, Robinson, one more mention

and you're sausage meat. Mention
us again and we'll twist out your heart
and you'll eat it,
we'll have your balls for a bow tie, Robinson,
you can write that down
if you need to, but breathe our name ...'

Don't mention the plan: new town, new name,
two fingers to those heartless bastards, and settle down.
There's a bus in the station. Go for it, Robinson.

Speaking Terms

This is not the blanket of night,
it is a poor advert for it.

Through the action of the wind
the clouds appear slashed, longwise,
into rough black shapes, like the remnants
of a poster stripped from a window.

We must be driving west because
the furthest hilltop cuts a broken line
against the fading light. Picturesque,
a talking point, except

words being what they are
we wouldn't want to lose the only sense
we can share in: silence.
I could say the clouds

are the action of our day
stopped here to evidence
the last four hundred miles
like a mobile, hardly moving.

But I ask you the time
and you tell me, in one word, precisely.

Going West

So from A to B
we point and counterpoint,
tread a thin line,
split hairs so finely

that we lose the thread.
With every manoeuvre you wonder
how I passed the test.
At every junction

I could fill in your face.
And with the temperature gauge
getting into the red, and at the invitation
of the Last Chance Service Station,

we pull up, let steam off
and give it a rest.
I'm so hungry
I could eat a buttered monkey. You,

you could manage a racehorse
and go back for the jockey.

A Few Don'ts about Decoration

Don't mope. Like Rome
it will not be built in a day,
unlike those raised barns
or Kingdom Halls we've heard of
with their pools of labour,

the elders checking
each side of the plumb-line,
the daughters and their pitchers of milk, full
beyond the brim. Their footings
are sunk before breakfast,

by sundown the last stone
is dressed and laid.
Don't let's kid ourselves, we know less
about third-degree burns
than we did about blowlamps. Don't forget:

it's three of sand to one of cement,
butter the tile and not the wall,
half a pound of spilt nails
will sweep clean with a magnet, soot
keeps coming and coming, sandpaper

smells like money.
Don't do that when I'm painting.
Don't begin anything
with one imperial spanner and a saw so blunt
we could ride bare-arse to London on it.

Also, when you hold down
that square yard of beech
and your eyes widen and knuckles whiten
as the shark's fin of the jigsaw blade
creeps inland . . .

don't move a muscle.
And don't you believe it: those stepladders
are not an heirloom but a death trap;
they will snap tight
like crocodile teeth with me on top

and a poor swimmer. Don't turn up
with till rolls like stair carpets. Don't blame me
if the tiles back flip from the wall
or the shower-head swallow-dives into the tub
and cracks it.

Don't give up hope
till the week arrives when *it's done*,
the corner turned, its back
broken, and everything comes on
in leaps and bounds

that even Bob Beamon would be proud of.
OK, that's a light-year away
but like a mountain – it's there.
Don't look down.
Don't say it.

Cultural Studies

She would put down the myth
of natural rhythm

with reference
to her cowrie-trading days

in the black, African interior.
How well she remembered

their poor playing
of her flageolet,

and their indifferent footwork
in the gentlemen's excuse-me.

Not the Furniture Game

His hair was a crow fished out of a blocked chimney
and his eyes were boiled eggs with the tops hammered in
and his blink was a cat flap
and his teeth were bluestones or Easter Island statues
and his bite was a perfect horseshoe.
His nostrils were both barrels of a shotgun, loaded.
And his mouth was an oil exploration project gone bankrupt
and his last smile was a caesarean section
and his tongue was an iguanodon
and his whistle was a laser beam
and his laugh was a bad case of kennel cough.
He coughed, and it was malt whisky.
And his headaches were Arson in Her Majesty's Dockyards
and his arguments were outboard motors strangled with fishing-
    line
and his neck was a bandstand
and his Adam's apple was a ball cock
and his arms were milk running off from a broken bottle.
His elbows were boomerangs or pinking shears.
And his wrists were ankles
and his handshakes were puff adders in the bran tub
and his fingers were astronauts found dead in their spacesuits
and the palms of his hands were action paintings
and both thumbs were blue touchpaper.
And his shadow was an opencast mine.
And his dog was a sentry-box with no one in it
and his heart was a first world war grenade discovered by
    children
and his nipples were timers for incendiary devices

and his shoulder-blades were two butchers at the meat-cleaving
    competition
and his belly-button was the Falkland Islands
and his private parts were the Bermuda triangle
and his backside was a priest hole
and his stretchmarks were the tide going out.
The whole system of his blood was Dutch elm disease.
And his legs were depth charges
and his knees were fossils waiting to be tapped open
and his ligaments were rifles wrapped in oilcloth under the
    floorboards
and his calves were the undercarriages of Shackletons.
The balls of his feet were where meteorites had landed
and his toes were a nest of mice under the lawn-mower.
And his footprints were Vietnam
and his promises were hot-air balloons floating off over the trees
and his one-liners were footballs through other peoples' windows
and his grin was the Great Wall of China as seen from the moon
and the last time they talked, it was apartheid.

She was a chair, tipped over backwards
with his donkey jacket on her shoulders.

They told him,
and his face was a hole
where the ice had not been thick enough to hold her.

Millet: The Gleaners

No one's twisting her arm but there it is,
locked backwards in a half-nelson, broken
like a shotgun. In hand, a spray of corn
spills out like a tail of peahen feathers.

The nearest is standing but bends also.
Like a forced branch or a trained limb, something
which has given, she curves, disarmed, a bow
without string hemmed in under the skyline.

The third shadows the first, and if the sunset
is a spotlight then she steals the finale
with a bow, not a curtsy. Past caring
she forgets the task, if it was picking
or planting, whether it was corn or barley.

Let me say this: we trip across the fields
like tourists; take flowers, tell huge stories –
lies, and think only of the poppies.
It could be midnight when the evening fades;

the hammock, the hats, the picnic basket,
the day like an apple – not even bruised
but somehow bottled, the road in sight, the car
where we left it. It will right itself, that square
of flattened grass where we laid the blanket.

Revision Exercise with Textbook Examples

To him, from
his side of the desk,
we were hatchlings in a cuckoo's nest,
every open mouth and wide eye intent on
the next fat scrap
of information.

But to us, gobstruck
behind screens and keyboards,
those bytes of hotspots, continental drift and lava bombs
were hard facts to swallow. Easy to see
but tricky to fathom
why Europe went East,

or how the ball
of North West Africa
tore from the socket of Central America,
or why that crack running round the Pacific
didn't lap up the ocean
and everything in it.

We still carried torches
for the perfect world, a globe
where things meant what they said, where the North Pole
was a cairn, or a crossroads, or an actual post
held tight in a tripod
of frozen ropes.

So, late one lesson
we were having a ball
that would have figured on the Richter scale,
and pinpointing me as the epicentre
he strode from the sunburst
of the overhead projector

and lost his grip,
and grabbed my hair,
and frogmarched me down to the Head of Year
who opened a file in the school computer
and saved an account
of the misdemeanour.

It was
just the beginning.
Later, in the walk-in freezer of the boys' gym,
I was sandwiched in a three-man slam dunk,
a breathtaking
stunt

which caught the eye
of a trained first-aider
whose famous cure for every ailment
was the laying on of hot dry hands
to the Y of his
patients' underpants.

Better, I was bundled back
to Geography, where
we recapped on the hemispheres,
and to grasp the Coriolis and Geostrophic forces
we took on board
a row of houses

which spanned the equator.
He sketched out a map:
at the northern end when they emptied the bath
the suds traced a spiral which left for the drainpipe
down a miniature whirlpool,
orbiting clockwise.

In the southern end-terrace
the bristles or tea leaves
in a sink or basin would mass like starlings
round the gulf of the plughole and be drawn
counter-clockwise through
a small anticyclone.

It needed no
chewing over. The water
in the house whose footings straddled the border
took its leave without fuss, straight down the middle
and not so much
as a single bubble.

Robinson's Statement

He could lie.
He could say
she'd been dead a month
when they dug out the hearth
and spuds were still in there,
cased in tinfoil,
still warm,
still tasty.

He could say
the icing-sugar bride and groom
were saved in cotton wool;
not crazed or nibbled
or parted or faded,
still swooning.

He could say
she slipped from this world to the next
like a rose dying back to its bud
or a tree in Autumn losing its last dry leaf.
He could lie about her teeth.

But the sergeant scuffed his boots
when he kicked the door down

and Robinson caught an eyeful: her dress
round her neck, her ancient underwear

soiled and irregular, the door
now over her, the sergeant on the door

like a big kid hogging the see-saw,
or that moment, how can he say this:

surfer and surfboard.

In Clover

This winter, six white geese have settled near the house.
This morning as she polishes the furniture
and peers across the river to their nesting place

she finds the gaggle floating off downstream, and there
instead is one white egg sat upright in the sand.
The geese, distracted with a crust, are unaware

as Rose, her eldest, in ankle socks and sandals
cradles the egg in the lap of her pinafore
and picks a safe way back across the stepping-stones.

She cracks the contents on a bed of cornflower
and paints policemen on the empty halves of shell
to sell as plant-pot-men in next month's flower show.

Later, the six white geese will crane their necks to smell
the fine egg-pudding cooling on the window-sill.

Without Photographs

We literally stumble over the bits
and pieces, covered with ash
and tarpaulin, stashed into corners,
all that tackle under the old mill.
I don't know how we finally figure it out,
poking around in the half-dark,
coming across the neatly coiled strips
of soft lead-flashing
and the fire-blackened melting equipment,
but it all fits together, falls into place.
For three weeks we light up the adapted oil-drum
with anything combustible:
door frames from the tip, spools, bobbins,
pallets, planks, old comics even which we sneak
from the house beneath our anoraks
and deliver on the run like parachute drops.

When we are forced to take a few steps backwards
and the heat stays in our faces like sunburn –
that's when the fire is hot enough.
We slide the melting-pot across the grill
(a stewing pan with no handle, a cooker shelf)
and toss in the lumps of lead
like fat for frying with. It doesn't melt
like butter, slowly, from the bottom upwards
but reaches a point where it gives up its form
the way the sun comes
strongly around the edge of a cloud.
Then it runs, follows the dints

in the pan, covers the base so we see ourselves –
an old mirror with patches of the back missing.
For moulds we use bricks.
Like stretcher-bearers we lift the pan
between two sticks then pour the fizzing lead
into the well of a brick.
Sometimes it splits it clean in half with the heat.

Today we watch the mould, prod it
through its various stages of setting, and can't wait
to turn it out like a cake, feel
its warm weight and read the brickwork's name
cast in mirror writing along its length.
But in the days that come, the shapes will mean less
and less, giving in to the satisfaction of the work.
What there is in the sweat, and the burns,
and the blisters, is unmistakably
everlasting. Not what is struck in the forged metal
but in the trouble we know we are taking.

And something about friends, walking home,
grinning like bandits, every pocket
loaded,
all of us black-bright and stinking like kippers.

Drawing the Arctic Circle

The last blizzard softens into sleet.
A certain heat gets under the shingle.
Glaciers rupture with the echo of metal.
Pack-ice is putting out to sea.

Arctic poppies bend in the breeze.
Bones sweat in the Eskimo middens.
Kelp slackens back to the meltwater-streams.
Atoms glitter in the solar wind.

Helen, you are the sweetest sister.
It's kind of you and Tom to offer.
Greenland is much as we imagined.
We've brought enough Scotch to sink the Titanic.

The stars seem almost close enough to touch.
God help us both if this is summer.
The sun shines all day and all night
but it has no warmth, no light, no colour.

Eighteen Plays on Golfing as a Watchword

I
Among the twenty lovers
of the Lady Captain, only one man

knew the wonder of an albatross.

II
At the second hole he saw the light,
paid off the caddie,
selected a nine iron and his favourite ball,

steered a clean shot through a gap in the wall
and followed it out onto the unmarked fairway

of the world.

III
Both our balls plugged
in that stodgy stuff
this side of the greenkeeper's hut.

You see them:
the mad eyes
of the ghost of the man in the mud.

IV

The flag and the green
from this elevation;

a heron in its pool
of stagnant water.

V

I was about to say something marvellous,
then forgot.

Oh yes,
I stood and was bamboozled
by a line of badger prints
which stopped in their tracks
at the heart of the sand-trap.

VI

You sliced a tee shot
off the toe of the club. It pinballed

through the copse, came back
to within spitting distance of where we stood,
and stopped.

A blackbird burst out laughing.

VII

To hole in one,

or at last let go of your boy
on his new bike as he makes it
the length of the drive, down the hill,
along the carriageway,
between the weighbridge and the bottle bank –
just a dot now –

and through the gates of the big school without falling.

VIII
Which fink blackballed the Captain's brother?

Among the twenty snow-white members
of the selection committee, the Captain's face

a picture.

IX
A three iron, two-hundred yards,
dead straight and a decent lie: one shot.

A sitter fluffed from two feet: one shot.

Not the fear of flying
but of falling.
Not the first ten-thousand feet
but the last one. Fatal.

X
An object-lesson in addressing the ball:

head down, hands
where you're happiest with them,
putter firm but at ease,
legs apart and slightly broken
at the knees.

You gents,
try it when you take a leak.

XI
Sometimes in bed I replay
every stroke
in that splendid round.

Some nights I dream
of badgers walking backwards.

XII
To do with film and shutter speed.
Just nicely teed off, this unremarkable old-timer
in a blurred imperfect circle,

caught in the act of his own swing.

XIII
Uncanny. On the thirteenth
a blackbird rears up
like an umbrella.

Rain begins to happen.

XIV

Us roughnecks from the council estate,
out before breakfast
thieving magic mushrooms from the practice fairway,
lost balls to flog at competitive prices
and song-thrush eggs from the rhododendrons.

From his hut,
over eighteen misty holes,
the greenkeeper turning a blind eye.

XV

Like a fish
it grows with every telling.

Yesterday you stroked it home from twelve yards.

Today you winkle it from the bunker;
it bites and borrows to the left, anchors up,
rattles the pin and somehow wangles its way in.

Plop.
Unforgettable.

XVI

I can't say which is preferable:

the fat man in his motorized buggy
getting no traction in that stodgy stuff
this side of the greenkeeper's hut,

or the lengthening shadow of the fat man
in his buggy, inching to the clubhouse
as he stays put.

XVII
The fairways deserted, the world's
our oyster.

In the wood the wind is the sound
of the sea.

A ball in the cup is a pearl
for the taking.

On the back nine, one fathom now
from the surface.

XVIII
Sundown, almost; the 19th
lit up like a petrol station.

Let's live for the moment.
For the hell of it let's tee one up
and belt it
into the nothingness.

A shooting star
agrees with us.

Robinson's Resignation

Because I am done with this thing called work,
the paper-clips and staples of it all.
The customers and their huge excuses,
their incredulous lies and their beautiful
foul-mouthed daughters. I am swimming with it,
right up to here with it. And I am bored,
bored like the man who married a mermaid.

And I am through with the business of work.
In meetings, with the minutes, I have dreamed
and doodled, drifted away then undressed
and dressed almost every single woman,
every button, every zip and buckle.
For eighteen months in this diving-helmet
I have lived with the stench of my own breath.

So I am finished with the whole affair.
As for this friendship thing, I couldn't give
a weeping fig for those so-called brothers
who are all voltage, no current. I have
emptied my locker. I should like to leave
and to fold things now like a pair of gloves
or two clean socks, one into the other.

This is my final word. Nothing will follow.

About His Person

Five pounds fifty in change, exactly,
a library card on its date of expiry.

A postcard, stamped,
unwritten, but franked,

a pocket-size diary slashed with a pencil
from March twenty-fourth to the first of April.

A brace of keys for a mortise lock,
an analogue watch, self-winding, stopped.

A final demand
in his own hand,

a rolled-up note of explanation
planted there like a spray carnation

but beheaded, in his fist.
A shopping list.

A giveaway photograph stashed in his wallet,
a keepsake banked in the heart of a locket.

No gold or silver,
but crowning one finger

a ring of white unweathered skin.
That was everything.